Like SYRUP over pancakes...

A journey shared

D1592457

Joanne Knox

All text and illustrations by the author.

ISBN 978-1-64471-113-2 (Paperback)
ISBN 978-1-64471-114-9 (Digital)

Copyright © 2019 Joanne Knox
All rights reserved
First Edition

Covenant Books, Inc.
11661 Hwy 707
Murrells Inlet, SC 29576
www.covenantbooks.com

To my beloved husband, Ron, who—more than anyone in my life—always encouraged me to be myself because that's who he fell in love with.

Contents

Preface

This is a love story of sorts, and it's a story of grief and growth and becoming. It has been a time of deep discovery for me. I found out things about myself as I navigated the grief that took hold of me when my husband, my true love and life partner of twenty-five years, became ill and died three weeks after his cancer diagnosis.

For a long time, nearly a year, I was learning how to live alone again as I grieved his loss and the loneliness that surrounded me. I was redefining my living space, making changes that represented who I was becoming as a single person, living alone in a home that I had shared for over twenty-five years.

I also had so much more time on my hands. I didn't enjoy cooking anymore. I didn't have anyone to cook for, anyone to enjoy it with. Although I have always been social and active in my community, the days just started to seem so much longer—the evenings, longer still.

That's when it happened—my passion for artistic expression rose up out of the depths of my very soul, catching me off guard and filling me with purpose again. It began as a ministry to beautiful and often hidden or marginalized women. It became a way for them to put on paper a representation of their feelings in such a way that they began to feel safe to talk about the emotion aroused by the topic we were describing through individual creative expression.

Painting and drawing became an obsession and a nurturing salve for my grieving heart. As I pursued a skill that I was told as a young girl I didn't have, I found a gifting and a joy I never knew existed within me, sitting there right alongside of my deep grief.

Women's faces, carrying many of the emotions I was feeling, began to emerge one after the other. As I sat with them, they became the representation of an emotion or feeling I had encountered as I navigated my grief.

Although the words and images represent my own journey, I suspect they also hold a bit of all women, those I know and those I do not. It has been for me an art and heart experience. My hope is that you will see my heart in my work and that the art and the words will, in some way, touch and delight you, perhaps give you hope.

As I left the room for this work to evolve, I found it becoming the devotional I had always believed I'd one day write. That day is here. My prayer for this book is that it will touch you in a way that only God could.

He has been at the center of all this book was meant to be and has become.

May reading it bless you as much as creating it has me.

At the end of the book, you will find blank pages left there for your own art and heart journey. Feel free to use them for journaling, for drawing, for creating your own "face" of whatever you are feeling at the moment. I encourage you to have a place, a treasure box perhaps, where you can save found strips of paper, ribbons, quotes, feathers and tiny stones and shells, all that you may find inspirational as you create your own works of art and heart.

In that way, you make this book yours, and that would bless me greatly! Give yourself permission to be imperfect because we all are. Remember this isn't so much about art as it is about expressing your own heart through your creativity.

Thank you for trusting me enough to open yourself to the words that follow.

In His grip,
Joanne

Acknowledgments

My deepest thanks and love to all of you who have walked with me through this time of loss and loneliness. Without your support, love, prayers, and encouragement, this book would have never emerged out of my darkest time.

Secondly, to the two extremely talented and gifted women, Ruth Gendler and Kelly Rae Roberts, whose words and art have inspired me to follow both my own creative heart and their beautiful styles.

To Glenn Livingston, an author himself, who by "chance" sat next to me on a plane one day and offered encouragement and support to bring this book to an audience who he believed would benefit from my words and art. He envisioned for me a much larger presence that I would have ever conceived of on my own.

To my dear friend, Mike Fornwald, himself an artist and creative force who gave me the title for this book.

To my very talented and gracious friend, Dena Ziebel, who spent so may hours in her basement office to add her visionary and photography gifts to creatively and artistically show-case the paintings of the women you see between the covers of this book.

And most deeply, my first love, Jesus Christ, who has carried me through it all.

Grace

Grace

Grace seems to just float into a room, the scent of lavender never far behind.

She knows what it feels like to be judged, to be misunderstood, to be singled out because of how others see her. She also knows how much it hurts.

When she hung out with Judgement and all of his friends, she found herself speaking in ways that were often hurtful and unkind. She seemed to always want revenge for the bad things people said about her. But she soon found out that revenge didn't fix anything, and it didn't make her feel any better either.

Then one day, Kindness sat down next to her, put her arms around her, and just let her pour out all the hurts and pain her little heart had been holding. When she was done, Kindness said to her, "None of this defines you. You are covered in a grace that no one can take away. All you need to do is receive it."

Grace couldn't believe her ears. She jumped up and began to twirl and sing in this new freedom she felt.

She felt free to not only receive the grace offered to her, but she could let it flow through her to others. That was the day she took her new name and the scent of lavender began to follow her everywhere.

For it is by grace that you have been saved through faith, and
this is not from yourselves, it is the gift of God.

—Ephesians 2:8

Despair

Despair can fall from the sky like a sudden winterstorm. She catches you off guard, leaving you without a blanket of protection and no place to run to escape her cold touch.

She can also linger like one of those dreary fall days, keeping you in her grip far longer than you had ever imagined being held by anyone—let alone her.

Despair often hangs out with Grief and Loneliness. And while she doesn't find comfort there, she is just too tired to walk away from them.

But sometimes, after her tears have watered the garden of her soul, and she looks inward to where her strength resides, she is surprised and grateful to find Hope sitting alongside of her, just quietly waiting with her as she endures the heaviness Despair brings. She feels blessed that she is no longer alone.

> Why my soul are you downcast? Why so disturbed within me? Put your
> hope in God, for I will yet praise Him, my Savior and my God.
>
> —Psalm 42:11

Lonesome

Loneliness

Loneliness can feel like shackles holding you back from even the simplest of tasks. Sitting in the space that used to feel like home, looking around at all the emptiness around you. Home seems so much less inviting than it did before loneliness moved in.

When she saw that you were now alone, didn't she move right in, take up residence, and make the space you inhabited feel so empty, so dreary, void of life outside of your own. She didn't help fill the space. She only made it feel emptier. She would often whisper to you, "You truly are alone, you'll always be alone, and this space you now live in alone, well it is just too big, too dark, too much."

But every once in a while, by God's grace, you were able to evade her dark embrace. In those sweet moments in the presence of others who understood and cared about how empty life must feel, Loneliness was forced to move out of the way, into the background, giving you room to breathe in freedom, and if only in those fleeting moments to feel alive again.

The Lord Himself goes before you and will be with you; He will never
leave you nor forsake you. Do not be afraid; do not be discouraged.
—Deuteronomy 31:8

Courage

Courage

Well, now, Courage has had a bit of experience with adversity in her day. Each time she overcame some obstacle that threatened to take her down, she found herself becoming stronger and more formidable. She actually looked a little taller.

As she faced obstacles, she did so as an overcomer, no longer fearful of what lay behind the mountain.

Courage has become best friends with her neighbor, Trust. Whenever they spend time together, talking about this and that, it seems that both of them are more able to stand on their own when facing tomorrow's surprises, secrets, and challenges. (Although they don't have to, they are best friends after all.)

Courage gets things done because she is even willing to do them afraid.

> This is my command—be strong and courageous! Do not be afraid or
> discouraged. For the Lord your God is with you wherever you go.
> —Joshua 1:9, NLT

> Be on guard. Stand firm in the faith. Be courageous. Be strong.
> —1 Corinthians 16:13, NLT

Patience

Patience

Patience knows the art of waiting. She has learned that most good and enduring things don't come quickly. Oh, she used to try to make things happen all the time, but then she learned that she couldn't always make things happen just because she thought they should. She could ask, she could teach, she could encourage, and sometimes she just had to be silent and wait. That was always the hardest—waiting.

Patience has also taken on the task of waiting for other people too. When their impatience drives them crazy, they turn to her quiet continence, and they are calmed and can sit with her awhile and wait.

She never seems irritated or disturbed. She just keeps moving forward with grace and contentment. Those three: Patience, Grace, and Contentment always seem to be together. Perhaps that is where Patience gets her strength to wait, even when it's hard, even when she wants it right now.

But in stillness, she waits graciously, knowing that goodness always comes to those who wait.

But if we hope for what we do not yet have, we wait for it patiently.
—Romans 8:25

Be joyful in hope, patient in affliction, faithful in prayer.
—Romans 12:12

Strength

Strength

Strength is very quiet about the power she has deep inside of her. She can stand before anyone without fear because she knows whose she is.

It wasn't always that way. She used to be friends with Defiance, and he had her confused about the difference between strength and selfishness. As she tired of all the conflict and strife in her life, she began to realize that she just might have the skills that she needed to navigate both the good and the bad in this world without it always being a fight. And so her friendship with Defiance drifted away, leaving room for new and better allies.

Soon she struck up a deep friendship with Kindness, Truth, and Honor. Her life is much happier now, and she is even stronger. Their friendships feed her, encourage her, and let her see the world in a whole different way. In fact, she acts more and more like them the longer they are friends.

> For I can do everything through Christ who gives me strength.
>
> —Philippians 4:13

He renews my strength. He guides me along right paths, bringing honor to his name.
> Psalm 23:3, NLT

compasssion

Walk in love, just as Christ also loved you and gave Himself up for us, an offering and a sacrifice to God as a fragrant aroma. Ephesians 5:2

Compasssion

Compassion

Compassion was born in the school of hard knocks. She has endured much grief, pain, and sorrow, yet somehow has been able to be present with others in the midst of their deepest distress.

I have learned so much in this season as she has sat quietly with me and listened to my tender heart. These are the things I've learned:

- You cannot offer another true compassion unless you have first experienced the things in life that touch you to the core.
- You can't offer another true compassion unless you yourself have first received compassion from another.

Then and only then can you put yourself inside another's pain and not be so impacted that you yourself get swallowed up by it. Compassion has been there, and she knows how to be with another and offer herself freely.

Compassion is a friend who comes and sits with you when you don't know what you need. She doesn't ask a lot of questions; she just sits with you and waits.

Clothe yourself with compassion, kindness, humility, gentleness, and patience.
—Colossians 3:12

Let us not love with words or speech but with action and in truth.
—1 John 3:10

Suffering

Suffering

Anyone who has been covered by the veil of suffering can look into her face and see the pain and distress she endures.

Suffering lives in a dark space, an alone space, one where light has to work really hard to penetrate. Light comes in the form of friends and kindness and mercy. Relief feels like a protective salve that covers a wound. As long as it remains intact, the wound doesn't hurt, but once it wears off, the pain and suffering return.

Suffering isn't all bad, you know. She brings with her a sense of dependence on others, which is how we were created to live. She also brings an openness to receive the grace and mercy offered by our Lord Jesus, who Himself suffered greatly and alone, giving us a model of dependence. He upon His Father, we upon Him. Suffering's best friend is Mercy. She comes over almost every day to spread a bit of protective salve on Suffering's heart wound. She makes Suffering's life just a bit more bearable and helps her to make it through one more day.

And the God of all grace, who called you to his eternal glory in Christ, after you have suffered a little while, will himself restore you and make you strong, firm, and steadfast.

—1 Peter 5:10

Anxiety

Anxiety

Anxiety has a really hard time standing still for very long. But once she realizes that she can't focus and that she can't even remember why she started moving in the first place, she stops moving on the outside, but her insides are moving at one hundred miles an hour.

There are other times when anxiety is paralyzed, unable to move, to reach out, to engage. Those times seem the hardest to her, spiraling her into a darkness that she can't crawl her way out of.

One day, I remember she told me that she stood for hours in front of a telephone that hung on the wall in the hallway. She just kept looking at it and couldn't command her hand to reach out, pick it up, and ask for help.

Thankfully, her roommate, Strength, came home before she had stood there too long and gave her the help she couldn't ask for.

Cast all your anxiety on Him because He cares for you.

—1 Peter 5:7

Cast your cares on the Lord and He will sustain you;
He will never let the righteous be shaken.

—Psalm 55:22

Faith

Faith

Faith is a beautiful woman who often wears flowers in her hair, rhinestones in her ears, and often appears to have her eyes closed. She hangs out with Grace and Compassion on a regular basis. Actually, they are some of her favorite people.

Faith doesn't ask for much, but she has much to offer to those who accept her as a friend. She is unafraid of the future or even the present moment because she knows her God and knows He has it covered whatever may come.

When she tells you that everything will be okay, she says it out of her own experience, and she means it with all her heart and soul.

To Faith, life is a beautiful adventure to be fully embraced without fear or regret. She is a gift to all those who call her friend.

Now faith is confidence in what we hope for and assurance about what we do not see.

—Hebrews 11:1

Hope

Hope

Hope, she is very much like Faith; in fact, they are good friends, often seen out and about together, laughing and looking for hidden treasures in secondhand shops. Hope, however, unlike Faith, walks through life with her eyes wide open and full of expectation.

There are a lot of things that she hopes for: for good things to happen for everyone, for love to always win out, that the lonely are noticed and cared for, that children never know abuse, that God's justice and mercy are evident to those who are watching. She never stops hoping, and Faith tells her not to because she knows that one day they will come true.

Mostly she hopes for peace and mercy to prevail in the hearts of all men.

"For I know the plans I have for you", declares the Lord, "plans to prosper
you and not to harm you, plans to give you a hope and a future."
—Jeremiah 29:11

Love

Love

Love has many friends. Faith, Hope, and Integrity are just a few of them. Because of her love of people and her gifting, she often invites them and others over for marvelous, lingering dinner parties.

Oh, they feast on the finest of foods and wines, and they feast on the love that flows from one to the other, to the other as they soak in the sweet hospitality that Love provides.

No one ever really wants to leave her home. They tend to linger long after the meal and the cleanup is done. Sometimes they just stay overnight because it is just too hard to leave. Besides Love has a beautiful collection of handmade quilts for them to wrap up in against the evening's cool breezes. Why would you ever want to leave Love's embrace?

And now these three remain, faith, hope and love. But the greatest of these is love.
—1 Corinthians 13:13

Come, let us drink deeply of love till morning; lets enjoy ourselves with love!
—Proverbs 7:18

Goodness

Goodness

She is one of those women that, when she sees your weariness, just can't help but cover you with a soft afghan that she just crocheted hours before. Looking into her eyes, your aching heart is eager to take in the tenderness she offers. As she holds your face in her hands and asks, "How are you, sweetie?" You know that she really wants to know.

On those days when everything seems too much, when there doesn't seem to be a future to hang on to because the past as you knew it is gone, she can lift you up out of that dreariness with her sweet kindness and care.

I happen to know that she is good friends with Compassion. I think they must spend a lot of time together because her goodness and kindness feels very much like Compassion's touch.

Surely goodness and love will follow me all the days of my life,
and I will dwell in the house of the Lord forever.

—Psalm 23:6

He will shield you with His wings.

He will shelter you with His feathers

His faithful promises ARE your armor and your protection.

Psalm 91:4

dreamer
friends
h you · h
ks · hella
est day
s · kind
t · brave
· become
re lovely
r heart
al · swee
ure · hi
eart · jo
elieve ·
e · great
love you
mily · h
smile ·
e · happy
k on you
ht · love
ether · h

Protection

Protection

She looks really brave, doesn't she? Facing away, perhaps turning her back on dangers that may lie somewhere on her path.

It's not so much that she is brave; she doesn't ever think of herself that way. She feels a shield of protection around her, a force, a benevolent spirit that hovers over, before, behind, and around her, keeping her safe from the unseen dangers in the heavenly realms. That protection gives her the strength she needs to face any of the dangers this world has to offer.

When you encounter her, you will see it on her face and sense it in her being. She is unafraid, unencumbered by the future. Her motto is, "I do not know what the future holds, but I know who holds my future."

> But let all who take refuge in you be glad; let them ever sing for joy. Spread your
> protection over them, that those who love your name may rejoice in you.
> —Psalm 5:11

INTEGRITY

Chin up, buttercup

"Integrity is built by defeating the temptation to be dishonest; humility grows when we refuse to be prideful; and endurance develops every time you reject the temptation to give up."   Rick Warren

Integrity

Integrity

Integrity can look you right in the eye no matter what needs to be said or done. She doesn't waver ever from the truth, nor will she walk away from an obligation or a friendship she has made.

If she says she loves you and is there for you, believe it! She does, and she is.

Integrity is the one you ask the hard questions of, like, "Does this outfit look good on me?" or "Was it wrong of me to ——?" because you know that she'll tell you the truth with great kindness. But she will tell you the truth. That's exactly the reason you ask her: you want the truth.

Do not be conformed to this world but be transformed by the renewing of your mind so that you may discern what is the will of God what is good and acceptable and perfect.
—Romans 12:2

May integrity and uprightness protect me, because my hope is in you.
—Psalm 25:21

"But blessed is the one who trusts in the LORD, whose confidence is in him. They will be like a tree planted by the water that sends out its roots by the stream. It does not fear when heat comes; its leaves are always green. It has no worries in a year of drought and never fails to bear fruit." Jeremiah 17:7-8

Contentment

Contentment

You can see it in her face, the peaceful way that she looks at you. Somehow you just know that she has mastered the art of not fretting over anything.

She walks around like one without a care in the world. Birds chirp as she passes by; butterflies swoop all around her as she meanders down the sidewalk on her way home from a day at the market.

She didn't find everything she was looking for. They didn't have any basil today. The apples looked good, but the tomatoes weren't quite ripe enough for her taste. So she went home without them but still had treasures in her basket that brought her joy.

She just doesn't fret. *Tomorrow is another day, and I have enough for this day. The sun is out, my health is good, and dinner will come with or without the basil.*

> I know what it is to be in need, and I know what it is to have plenty.
> I have learned the secret of being content in any and every situation,
>   whether well-fed or hungry, whether living in plenty or in want.
> —Philippians 4:12

Trust

Trust

Trust always seems to have a smile on her face, and a kind and encouraging word to offer. Her eyes slant heavenward because she trusts in Him.

Oh, she has had her fair share of stormy seas, shifting patterns in her life, disappointments, losses, and horrible things that have come out of the blue without warning. But still she stands on solid ground, trusting that she will not be swallowed up by life's unpredictable left turns.

Her sister, Faith, has been a great help and comfort to her when life does feel overwhelming and the unpredictable takes her off course. Faith lifts her up, reminds her of His promises, and sits with her until the storm passes, and it always passes.

I guess that's why, even in the eye of the storm, Trust still has a smile on her face and a kind and encouraging word to offer. Faith has helped Trust be able to stand on a firm foundation.

You will keep in perfect peace those whose minds are steadfast because they trust in you.
—Isaiah 26:3

Worthy

Worthy

She is quiet, shy, and quite reserved, often needing to be reminded just what her name means. There were so many things that happened to her in her young life that she grew up believing the lies that she was unlovable, somehow just not quite enough. I have to remind her that she doesn't earn it, she can't lose it, and she doesn't tarnish it by anything that she says or does—she just is Worthy.

That's how the Creator sees her; that's what He named her: *Worthy*.

Sometimes still, now that she has grown older, other people can say or do things to her that make her question the truth of her worthiness. She forgets that she was made worthy once and for all when Jesus chose to stand in the gap between sin and God. No one has the power to take away from her what He freely gave.

So long as she holds that truth in her heart, she is free to live in the glory of her name Worthy.

And all are justified freely by His grace through the redemption that came by Christ Jesus.
—Romans 3:24

Welcome her in the Lord as one who is worthy of honor among God's people.
—Romans 16:2

you & me

you are enough for me

Thinking of you today

How sweet all at once it was for me to be rid of those fruitless joys which I had once feared to lose! You drove them from me, You who are The true, the sovereign joy. You drove them from me and took their place, You, who are sweeter than all pleasure. —Augustine

PLEASURE

Pleasure

46

Pleasure

Pleasure, oh sweet pleasure! She can flow out of nowhere and side all over you like syrup over pancakes.

The thing about pleasure is that she is never in a hurry. She wants to experience everything and everyone she encounters fully, deeply, completely.

I wonder, have you ever watched her eat an ice-cream cone? She takes a long time choosing just what flavor might suit her today. Then she gazes at that cone for just a bit before she lets her tongue leisurely slides across the top. Holding the ice cream in her mouth, taking in every nuance of its flavor, you stand spellbound by her total surrender to the experience. You watch as the drips form and slide down the cone onto her fingers, dropping onto the ground beneath her. That's how she does life too!

Once you have experience pleasure's embrace, you can't really live fully anymore without her. She is like a sweet, slightly cool breeze of summer that sneaks up under your blouse and secretly caresses your skin.

> When the Lord takes pleasure in anyone's way, He causes
> their enemies to make peace with them.
>
> —Proverbs 16:7

her
name is
grateful
she is
the
guardian
of
contentment

Grateful

48

Grateful

Grateful has found many things and people in her long life to be thankful for. Looking back over her many years, she knows that in this life, she has been blessed beyond measure by the people and circumstances she has met along life's path.

Each morning, as is her routine, she steps out her front door, looks at the sky and the beautiful vistas before her, and she is filled with gratitude for life itself.

Sometimes it is sunny, and sometimes there are only clouds in the sky. It matters not. She even finds joy in the rain, embracing its cleansing beauty. It seems that nothing much happens in her day that she doesn't lift her eyes to heaven and thank God for her blessed life.

Her grateful spirit has created a contented heart. She has learned to be content no matter what the circumstances. As she considers her long life and all the love she has experienced within it, she lives each day satisfied and surrendered, knowing that she has received all the blessing she needs and far more than she could have ever asked for.

The boundary lines have fallen for me in pleasant places;
surely I have a delightful inheritance.

—Psalm 16:6

Whimsy

Whimsy

Poor Whimsy, she gets misunderstood so much of the time. People tend to speak of her as just a little bit strange. She surely is different from most people I know. Sadly some unkind people even go so far as to say that she is "a little left of center," if you know what I mean.

Truth is, in reality, she is a free woman. Free to be herself, free to try new things, free to experience people deeply. She is unencumbered by all of the "shoulds" of this world, and she doesn't impose that standard on anyone else.

That's why, even though she may stand out in her unique spirit and appear a little different, people are still drawn to her and her sense of freedom and peace. They can't help themselves. Captivity knows freedom when it shows itself.

> You are the light of the world. A city built on a hill cannot be hid. No one after lighting a lamp puts it under the bushel basket, but on the lampstand, and it gives light to all in the house. In the same way, let your light shine before others so that they may see your good works and give glory to your Father in Heaven.
> —Matthew 5:14–16

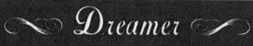

Dreamer

Dreamer

We all know the fruit of Dreamer. We dream whether we are awake or asleep. Daydreams are the best. They are her favorite too because they can take her away from boredom like a redundant office meeting into a magical place of her own design, where everything is perfect and beautiful.

Dreamer can become your best friend or your worst enemy depending on what she brings as you sleep. Sometimes she wakes you up too soon when you were just getting to the good part. Darn! Other times, she feels cruel, as she lets you wander around, lost in places you don't know, struggling to find your way out, and you never do. Instead, you wake up with an uneasy feeling, disoriented, maybe a little anxious. Then you remember the dream. Thank goodness, it was only a dream!

There is another aspect to Dreamer. Some call it wishing, some call it wanderlust. She calls it the beginning of finding your way to the life you have always wanted. Without our dreams, our hopes, our desires, life can stay pretty flat. Dreamer says, "Go ahead, dream, imagine, set some goals. Grow into a place where you are excited to wake to a new day and set your sail toward the tomorrow you always wanted."

Each of us had a dream the same night, and each dream had a meaning of its own.
—Genesis 41:11

Amid disquieting dreams in the night, when sleep falls on people,
fear and trembling seized me and made all my bones shake.
—Job 4:13–14

Death

Death

Death... look at her. She is so peaceful, so serene, ready for what lies beyond the veil. I think I know why. It's because she knows where she is going. She knows that she is going home.

For those of us still here, still living, it is hard to fathom what some other life might look like. We no doubt have many questions:

> Is there a heaven? Where is it then?
> Will it look anything like here?
> Surely we'll not be floating on clouds, right?
> Will we know people there?
> An on and on it goes.

So you know when you're taking a trip or driving someplace for the first time, that GPS on your phone or in your car takes all the stress out of the trip, doesn't it? Well, it's like that with death. You have a GPS for that too. The Bible and Jesus's words spoken to us tell us clearly where we are going, what it will be like, and who will be there with us.

I don't know about you, but that gives me peace. Just like Death's face, mine can be serene in my faith and assurance of what tomorrow brings.

> Those who walk uprightly enter into peace, they find rest as they lie in death.
> —Isaiah 57:2

For the wages of sin is death, but the gift of God is eternal life in Christ Jesus our Lord.
—Romans 6:8

The following pages are for your
art and heart journey.